Spaceship Earth

Gina Dal Fuoco

Earth and Space Science Readers:
Spaceship Earth

Publishing Credits

Editorial Director
Dona Herweck Rice

Associate Editor
Joshua BishopRoby

Editor-in-Chief
Sharon Coan, M.S.Ed.

Creative Director
Lee Aucoin

Illustration Manager
Timothy J. Bradley

Publisher
Rachelle Cracchiolo, M.S.Ed.

Science Contributor
Sally Ride Science

Science Consultants
Nancy McKeown,
Planetary Geologist
William B. Rice,
Engineering Geologist

Teacher Created Materials
5301 Oceanus Drive
Huntington Beach, CA 92649
http://www.tcmpub.com
ISBN 978-0-7439-0565-7

Printed by: 51497
Printed in: China

Table of Contents

Our Spaceship

Think of Earth as a giant spaceship. It is traveling though space. While it travels, it supports every living thing on it.

When **astronauts** travel into space, they must take everything they need with them. They bring food and water. They bring air to last

for the length of their voyage. If they are not careful, they may run out of what they need to survive.

Humans on Earth must be careful, too. The Spaceship Earth is made of parts that supply us with air, water, and food. If those parts stop working, our voyage may not last very long.

How Fast Are We Traveling?

Earth is moving through space at 20.8 kilometers (18.5 miles) every second. That is 1,200 kilometers (750 miles) in one minute.

Mission Specialist Kathryn Sullivan looks out the window of the space shuttle to Earth below.

What Is Our Spaceship Made

There are three basic parts to Earth. The first is the **atmosphere.** This is a gas shell. It surrounds the planet. It protects us from the sun. It also contains our air supply. The atmosphere is like the metal body of a spaceship that protects the astronauts and their supplies.

The next part is the **hydrosphere.** This is all the water on the planet. The hydrosphere includes our oceans, lakes, rivers, streams, and clouds. The water is like the spaceship's water and food supply.

Spaceship Earth has three important parts. They all make up the biosphere.

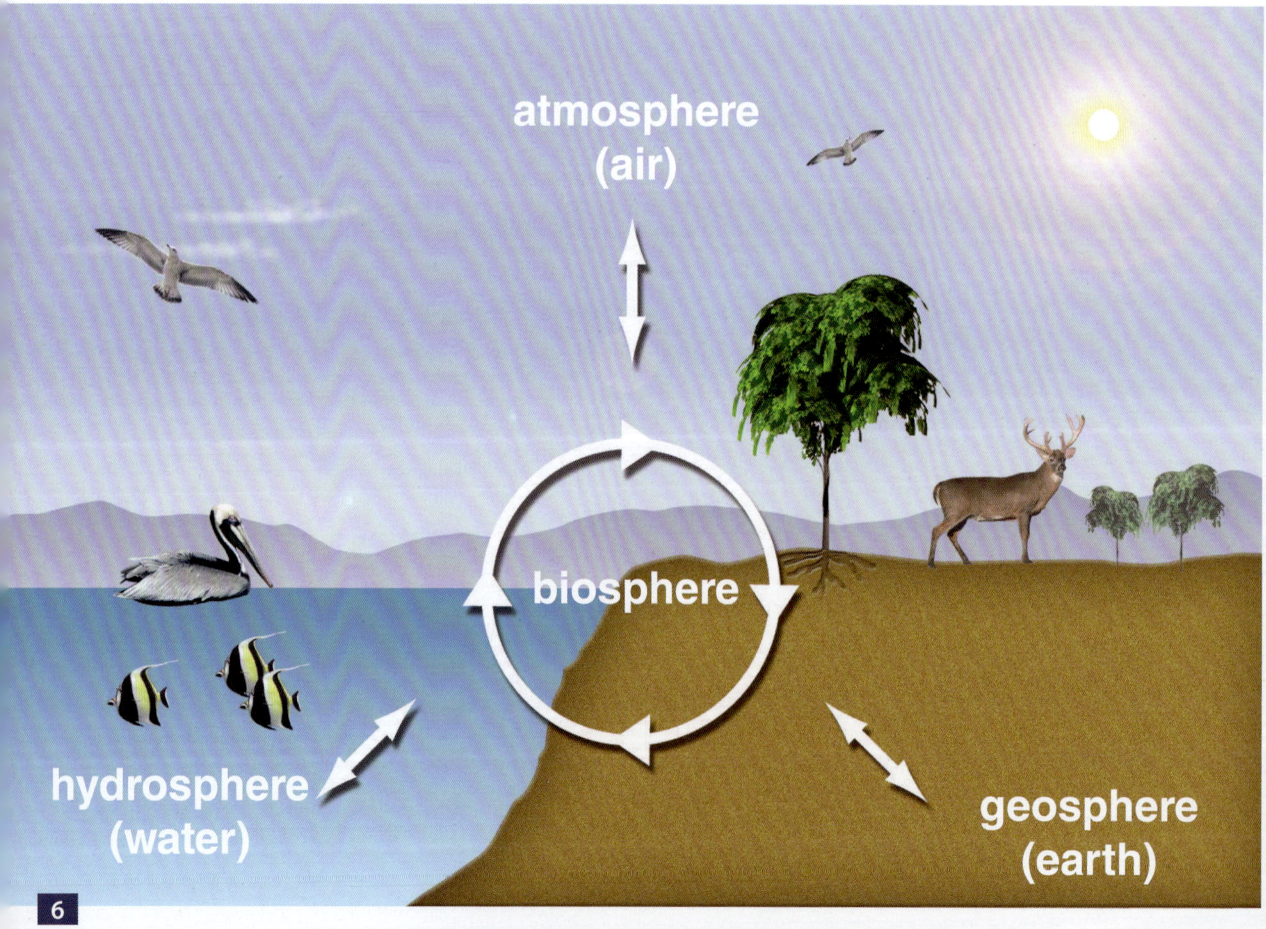

Of?

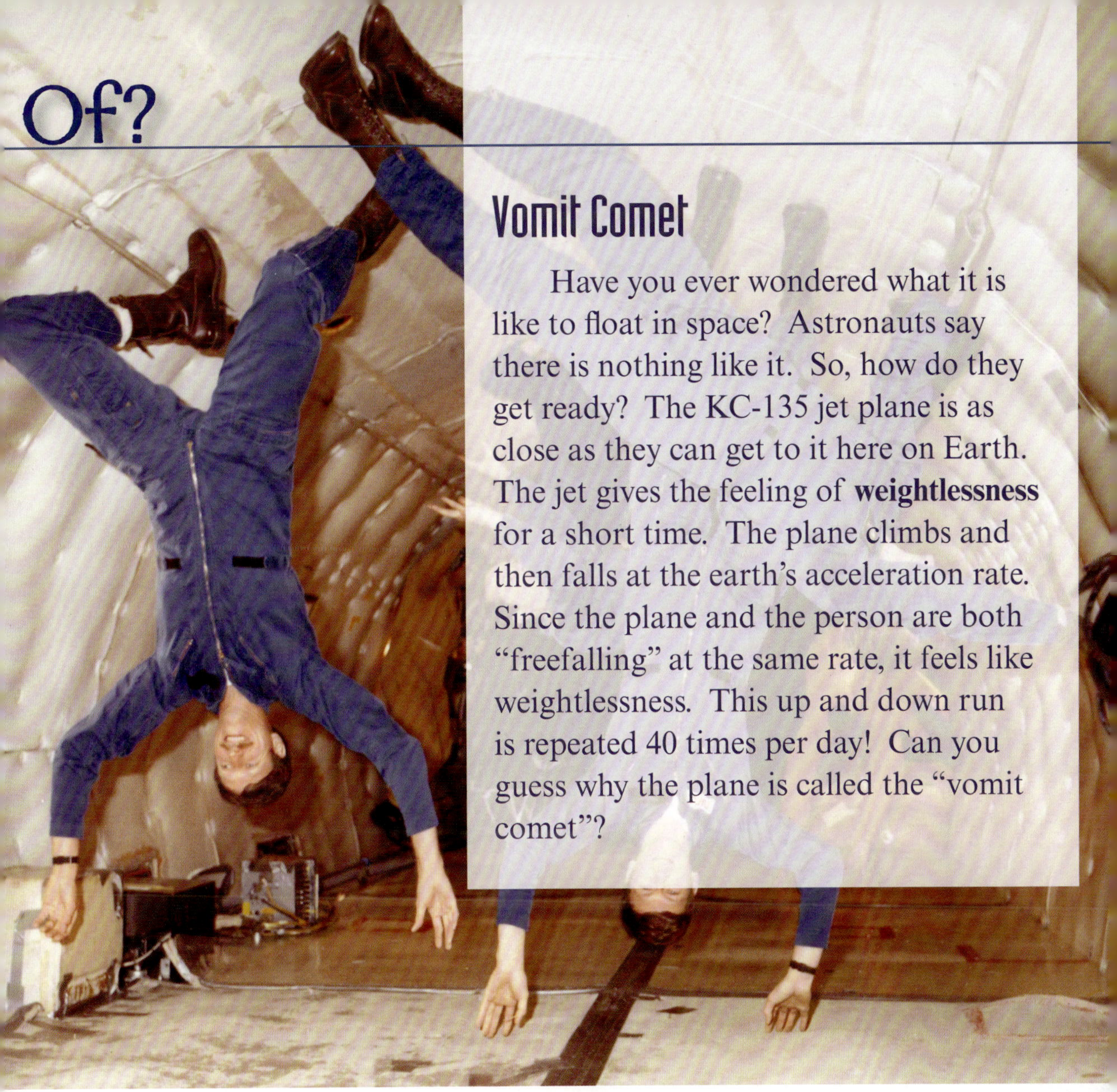

Vomit Comet

Have you ever wondered what it is like to float in space? Astronauts say there is nothing like it. So, how do they get ready? The KC-135 jet plane is as close as they can get to it here on Earth. The jet gives the feeling of **weightlessness** for a short time. The plane climbs and then falls at the earth's acceleration rate. Since the plane and the person are both "freefalling" at the same rate, it feels like weightlessness. This up and down run is repeated 40 times per day! Can you guess why the plane is called the "vomit comet"?

The third part is the **geosphere,** the rocks. It is mainly made up of just 12 elements. This is the spaceship's structural frame.

These three parts are all working together to keep Earth going. Can you imagine if one of these things were missing? What would happen if our spaceship didn't have all these parts and supplies?

A Bird's-Eye View

Do you like to travel? Do you take pictures when you visit someplace new? If you were traveling in space, what pictures would you want? We have learned a lot about Earth from space travel. The pictures taken from space tell us about weather. They tell us about our **environment** and ocean **currents**.

Satellites are like eyes in space. They can take pictures of the earth. The pictures warn us of big storms. They also help experts check changing weather patterns. Satellites help us see how the planet is changing over time. The pictures show us how we are changing the planet. These changes are both good and bad.

This illustration depicts a satellite above Earth.

Sally Ride on the space shuttle *Challenger*.

What Will the Weather Be Today?

Pictures from space are used every day to predict the weather. This is very helpful when big storms are on the way.

An Astronaut's View

In 1983, Sally Ride became the first American woman to travel in space. She was 200 miles above the earth. She could see the atmosphere. Dr. Ride took pictures of our planet from the space shuttle.

Over the years, others have followed her lead. Astronauts have taken more than 350,000 color photos. They wanted people to look at their pictures. They hoped people could learn a lot about how Earth works from these pictures.

A Planet Under Pressure

Everything in a spaceship is connected. Astronauts cannot live without all of it. They need the air and food. They need the water and the protection of their spaceship.

The three parts of Earth are closely connected, too. The winds in the atmosphere control how the ocean currents move. The ocean currents move water around the world. The water then makes our weather change. If it rains too much or too little, this affects the people and animals living on land. So, if we do not take care of one part of Earth, such as the ocean, we are really hurting the entire planet.

The ocean contains a great variety of life.

Did You Know?

The atmosphere is more than 150 kilometers (93 miles) thick. But most of the air is in the 42 kilometers (26 miles) closest to Earth.

The ocean is an important part of Earth. Yet many people think very little about it. Life on Earth would not exist without the ocean. Organisms living in the ocean give us a great deal of the oxygen that we breathe. Oceans hold 97 percent of the water on Earth. The ocean also takes in **carbon dioxide** made by humans. It gives us fresh water through clouds. Imagine if all that stopped happening. Life on Earth would disappear.

The sun keeps our spaceship running.

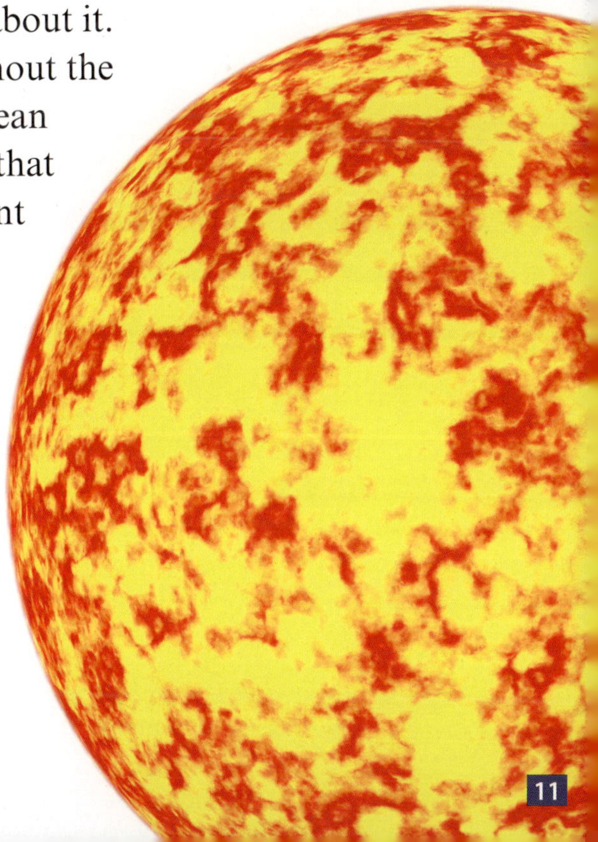

In fact, some life forms are disappearing. Dinosaurs disappeared from Earth thousands of years ago. We are now in danger of losing more life forms.

Biodiversity is the combination of all the different plants and animals in the world. The mix of plants and animals provides us with everything we need for **survival**. We all need and share water, air, and shelter. Living things are connected to each other. Losing one plant or animal can harm others. To protect our biodiversity, we must stop the high rate of loss of plants and animals.

Every living thing on Earth needs other living things to survive.

Fill It Up with T-Rex

Many people believe that oil comes from dinosaurs. This is close, but not quite right. Sometimes dinosaurs and the plants of their time died and the remains did not break down normally. They could have been trapped in a tar pit or buried under ash. They were squeezed and heated underground. They might have turned into **peat** on the surface and become buried underground. Then the peat turned into coal. Today, both peat and coal are used as energy sources for heating and producing electricity.

The story is different in the ocean. When dinosaurs in the water died, they sank to the bottom along with plants and algae. They were covered by sand and rocks. They were squeezed and heated underwater for even longer. Eventually, the remains turned into crude oil and natural gas.

Dinosaurs no longer walk the earth. They have become extinct.

Exploiting Earth's Resources

Earth offers everything we need for survival, including sources of energy. The trick is to use what Earth offers without damaging the planet in the process.

Oil is one of Earth's natural resources. It is pumped from deep inside the earth and then used to make many things. Oil is a valuable source of **energy**. We use this energy to drive our cars. We also use it to heat our homes and to run factories. Oil is not a clean source of energy. When we make it and use it, we are polluting Earth. Not only that, but we are using much more oil than Earth can make.

Pump jacks or "nodding donkeys" bring oil up from under the ground.

So How Much Oil Is Left?

The world's oil reserves are at around 1,200 to 1,300 billion barrels. That is enough oil to last only 45 more years.

There are other kinds of energy that we can use. They are renewable. This means they can be made over and over again. For example, the sun releases energy every day. This is a cleaner form of energy, and we have a never-ending supply. Wind also is clean energy. Scientists are even looking at ways to turn water into energy for cars. Using these other forms of energy will help keep our planet healthy.

The e4 from Global Electric Motorcars is an energy-efficient, electric car.

Wind turbines like these may provide your power in the future.

Permanent Damage?

What would happen if our spaceship were damaged? Would we still be able to fly, or would we come crashing down? How would we survive?

Sadly, Earth has been damaged. Some of this damage may not be able to be fixed. One example is **global warming**. Global warming is an average increase in Earth's surface temperature. In other words, Earth is hotter than in the past. Some of this is happening naturally. But the planet is getting warmer for another reason. There are **greenhouse gases**. Some

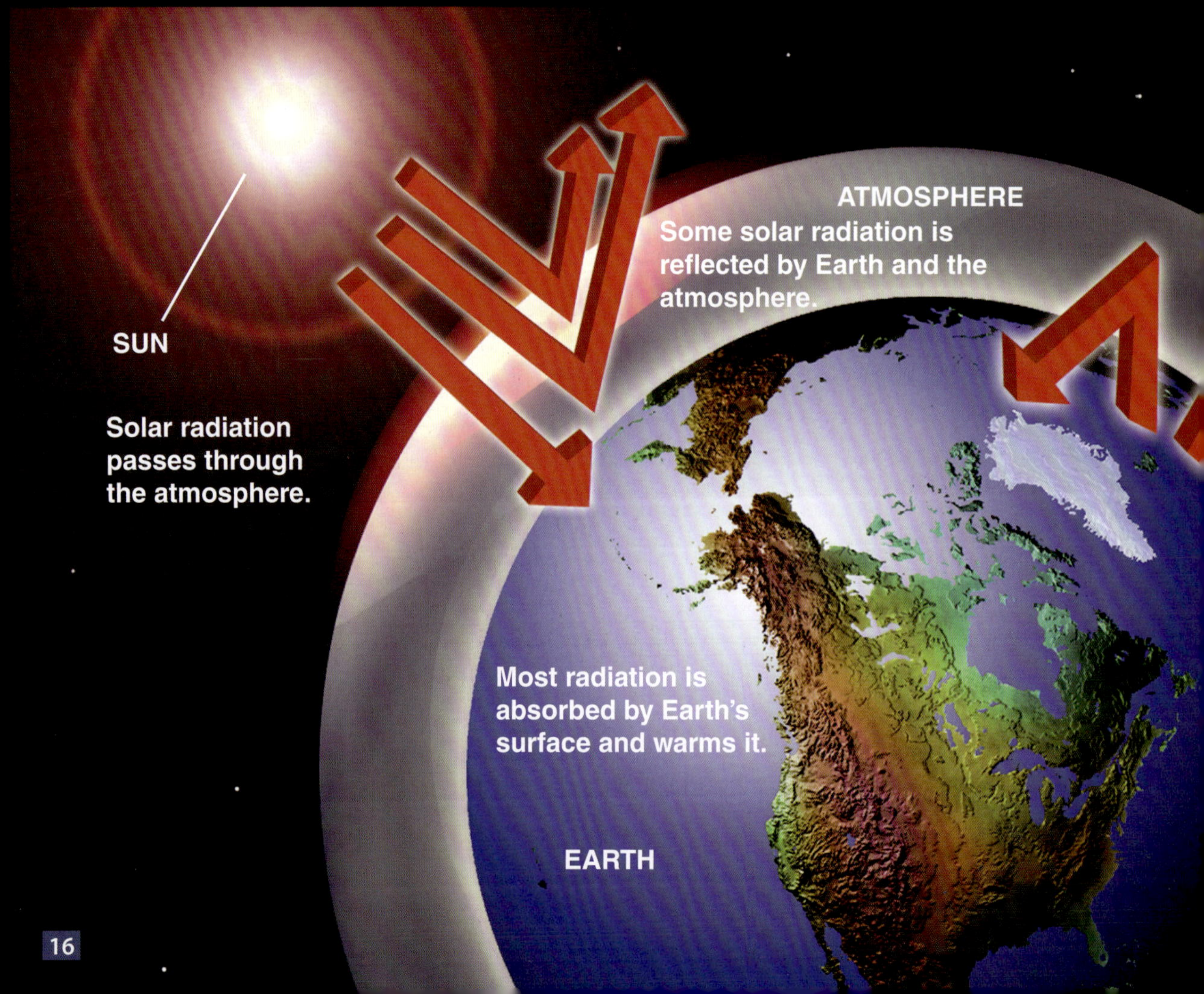

of these gases are made from natural things like breathing. They also are created by **pollution** from things such as cars and factories.

Scientists worry about Earth's temperature getting warmer. Many scientists predict that we will see serious side effects. One side effect is a change in normal weather.

This may cause low rainfall in some places. It may cause warmer weather in other places. It might cause floods or droughts. It might cause an increase in insects and rising sea levels.

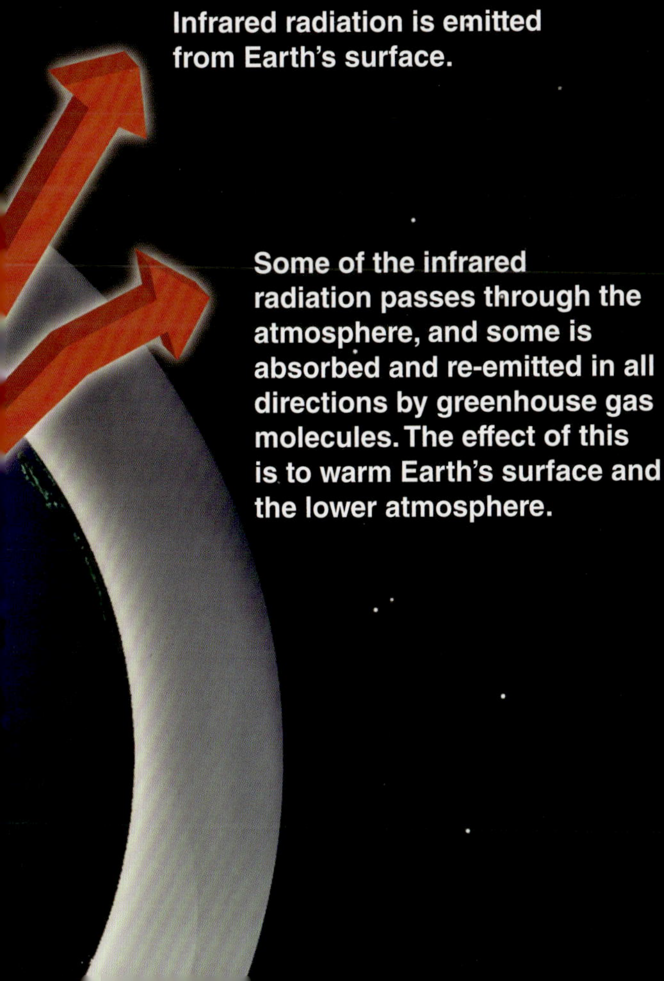

Arctic Sea ice, 1979

Arctic Sea ice, 2003

Acid rain is another cause of damage to the planet. It happens when acid from air pollution falls out of the atmosphere. It falls as rain, fog, or snow. The acid goes into the ground, ocean, and other bodies of water. If the acid level is very high, it can harm plant and animal life. **Marine life** is often the first to show signs of damage from acid rain.

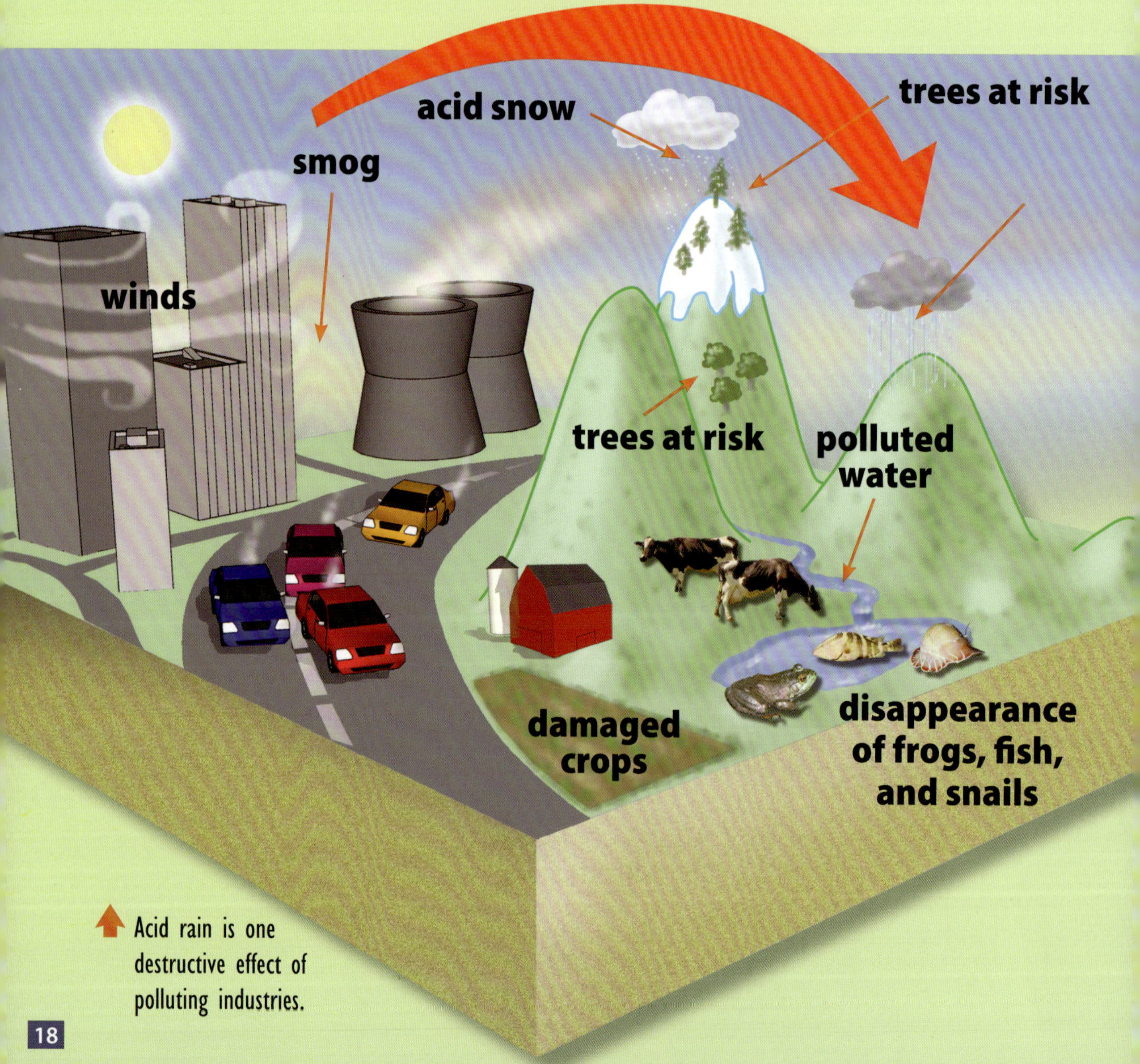

Acid rain is one destructive effect of polluting industries.

Workers who harvest chicle are called chicleros.

Save the Gum Forest

Do you like to chew gum and blow bubbles? You can thank the rainforest for that treat. Gum was first made out of chicle. Chicle is tree sap. It is found on a tree in the rainforest. The sap is boiled. It turns into a rubber-like material. Then it is mixed with sugar and flavorings.

Today gum companies make gum differently. They have found a way to make a man-made gum base. They don't use chicle. The good thing about chicle, though, is that it is a renewable resource. Using chicle gives people a way to make money without cutting down trees. There are a few companies who still make gum the old-fashioned way. They are helping the rainforest and gum lovers, too!

Up in Smoke

Twenty percent of all greenhouse gases come from rainforest destruction. When rainforests are cut and burned, gases are emitted. Also, with fewer trees, less carbon dioxide is used up.

Deforestation is another way in which Earth has been damaged. This happens when large areas of forest are cut or burned down. The loss of trees creates many problems. Trees take the carbon dioxide out of the air. Then they give us clean oxygen that we need for our air supply.

The forest is also important when it comes to rain. Tree leaves catch water from the air. Tree roots help water soak deep into the ground. Fallen branches and leaves keep water from flowing downhill. Without trees, the areas that were once forest become very dry.

These changes in the Earth will likely affect people on Earth. They might lead to poor health and lower economic development.

Whole cities can be affected by deforestation.

This satellite image shows deforestation in the Brazilian rainforest.

Human Responsibility

The whole planet must get involved to keep our Spaceship Earth running smoothly.

So what are people doing to keep Spaceship Earth going on its journey? Many countries are working together. They want to slow down some of the damage. In 1997, many world leaders met. They worked on solutions to reduce the amount of greenhouse gases we put into the air. The nations made a promise to reduce greenhouse gases. Some nations kept their promises, but not others. In the U.S., the changes were not made into laws.

Earth is a living system. It is normal for it to be changing. But many scientists are worried about how quickly Earth is changing. Some of the changes are not reversible. It is going to take the whole world working together to make lasting change for the better.

French Polynesia's coral reefs are lively and colorful, but they may be damaged by global warming.

Lost Beauty

In 1998, the beautiful Rangiroa Atoll coral reefs in French Polynesia died. It was due to global warming. The damage was bad. Experts say it will take more than 100 years to return the reefs to their former beauty. Divers like to see all the wildlife in the lagoon. For now, they can see all the damage, too.

What would happen if astronauts ate more food than they had on their spaceship? They would have nothing left for the rest of their trip.

The same is true with Earth. We are using more of Earth's supplies than we have onboard. We know our supplies are low. We must make changes. If we keep polluting our air and overusing our water supply, our voyage will end. We must think of new ways to save and **recycle** our supplies. Every crew member must be responsible for his or her usage. When we use more than we need, we are taking away from others. This creates an imbalance in nature.

The average American produces four and a half pounds of trash a day.

We face a big challenge. How do people think about the well-being of our planet? For thousands of years, we have used what we wanted from Earth. We haven't put much back. But the choices we make every day affect our planet and its survival.

Who Said it?

"We cannot solve the problems that we have created with the same thinking that created them." That was said by the famous scientist Albert Einstein.

Instead of throwing things out, we can recycle and reuse the materials so they are not wasted.

What Can You Do?

One person cannot reverse all the damage done to Earth. So, why bother? Because you can make a difference! You can choose to recycle your soda can or your water bottle. You can buy things made from recycled products.

Or you can make the easiest choice of all. Decide how to travel to school, if you can. Walking or riding your bike will keep our air cleaner. If all the six billion people on Earth make better choices, we can make a difference!

Riding your bike instead of driving creates less pollution—and it's fun!

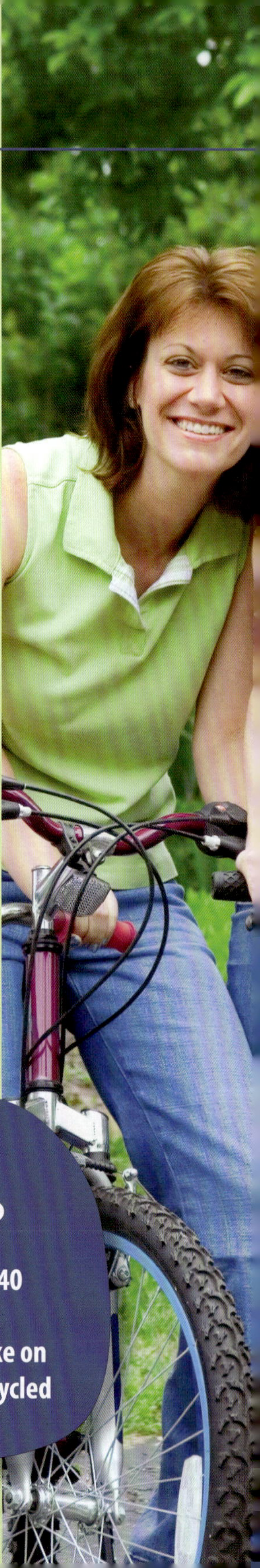

What's in Your Trash?

Paper products make up about 40 percent of our trash. Just think what a difference we could make on Spaceship Earth if everyone recycled all the paper.

Is That a Soda Bottle You're Wearing?

What happens to those soda bottles once you drop them in the recycle bin? Some companies turn them into shoes. In 1991, a small company made the first shoe from recycled materials. They use soda bottles, magazines, plastic milk jugs, coffee filters, and much more. It doesn't stop there. Don't put those recycled shoes in the trash when you're done. The company has found a way to re-recycle them, too! This got the attention of some big shoe companies. Now, big brands such as Adidas and Nike are trying to find new ways to use old stuff.

Lab: Acid Rain

This lab will explore the effects of acid rainfall on buildings and statues.

Materials

- clear glass
- six pieces of chalk (not the dustless type)
- water
- small bowl
- vinegar
- notebook and pencil
- clear carbonated drink (lemon-lime soda or sparkling water)
- lemon juice

Procedure

1. Put one piece of chalk in the glass and add water so that the chalk is completely covered.
2. Put a second piece of chalk in the bowl and add enough vinegar so that the chalk is completely covered.
3. Observe the chalks for a few minutes for any changes. Then leave overnight.

4 On day two, record what you see. Do you see gas bubbles in the glass of chalk and water? Are there gas bubbles in the bowl with the vinegar? Where are the bubbles coming from?

5 Repeat the lab with a clear, carbonated drink. Is the carbon dioxide in the soda enough to break down the chalk?

6 Pour lemon juice over one piece of chalk and vinegar over another until the chalk breaks down. What is more acidic—lemon juice or vinegar?

Conclusion

Many old buildings and statues are made from marble, limestone, and sandstone. These materials have large amounts of calcium carbonate, which is also found in some brands of chalk. The acid in the rain can wash off part of the surface of buildings made with these materials. It can also cause corrosion on things made of metal such as cars and bridges. All rainwater is a little bit acidic. However, when rain is very acidic from the effects of pollution, it can do damage.

Glossary

acid rain—acid precipitation falling as rain, fog, or snow

astronauts—a person trained to pilot, navigate, or participate as a crew member of a spacecraft

atmosphere—the whole mass of air surrounding the earth

biodiversity—the combination of all the different plants and animals on the planet

carbon dioxide—a gas with no smell or color that is made as a product of breathing and decomposition, or is released from volcanoes or burning things made of hydrocarbons

currents—the part of the ocean or a body of water that has a continuous onward movement

deforestation—the destruction of forests by people

energy—a source of usable power, such as petroleum or coal

environment—the combination of physical conditions that affect and influence the growth, development, and survival of organisms

geosphere—the rocky part of the earth

global warming—the increase in temperature near Earth's surface caused by polluting gases such as carbon dioxide

greenhouse gases—about 30 gases created by human activity, the main one being carbon dioxide; they contribute to the greenhouse effect

hydrosphere—the waters of the earth's surface

marine life—things relating to the sea or ocean

peat—compact vegetable matter used as fuel

pollution—the act or process of contaminating the soil, water, or the atmosphere

recycle—sorting and reprocessing old material into new usable materials

survival—to stay alive or in existence even through hardships

weightlessness—having little or no weight

Index

Sally Ride Science

Sally Ride Science™ is an innovative content company dedicated to fueling young people's interests in science. Our publications and programs provide opportunities for students and teachers to explore the captivating world of science—from astrobiology to zoology. We bring science to life and show young people that science is creative, collaborative, fascinating, and fun.

Image Credits

Cover: NASA; p.3 NASA; p.4 NASA; p.4–5 NASA; p.5 Andrea Danti/Shutterstock; p.6 (top) Ralf Juergen Kraft/Shutterstock; p.6 Tim Bradley; p.7 NASA; p.8 (top) NASA; p.8 (bottom) Andrea Danti/Shutterstock; p.8–9 NASA; p.9 NASA; p.9 (background) NASA; p.10 (top) Natalia Bratslavsky/Shutterstock; p.10 (bottom) Dennis Sabo/Shutterstock; p.11 (top) ANP/Shutterstock; p.11 (bottom) Michael Lawlor/Shutterstock; p.12 (top left) Kevin Swope/Shutterstock; p.12 (top right) Jose Manuel Rodrigues de Oliveira Costa/Shutterstock; p.12 (bottom left) Luís Alexandre Santos Louro/Shutterstock; p.12 (bottom right) Zygimantas Cepaitis/Shutterstock; p.12–13 (top) Kateryna Potrokhova/Shutterstock; p.12–13 (bottom) Anastasiya Igolkina/Shutterstock; p.13 (top) Denis Tabler/Shutterstock; p.13 (bottom) Tyler Olson/Shutterstock; p.14 (top) iStockphoto; p.14 (bottom) Jason Smith/Shutterstock; p.15 (top) Pattie Steib/ Shutterstock; p.15 (bottom) iStockphoto; p.16 (top) Daniel Bendjy/iStockphoto; p.16 (bottom) Tim Bradley; p.16–17 Tim Bradley; p.17 (top) NASA/Photo Researchers, Inc.; p.17 (bottom) NASA/Photo Researchers, Inc.; p.18 Tim Bradley; p.19 (background) Edward Parker/Alamy; p.19 Todd Taulman/Shutterstock; p.20 (top) Mark Atkins/Shutterstock; p.20 NRSC/Photo Researchers, Inc.; p.21 Edward Parker/Alamy; p.22 (top) Martin Strmiska/Shutterstock; p.22 (bottom) NORMAND BLOUIN/AFP/Getty Images; p.23 Westend61/Alamy; p.24 ImageState/Alamy; p.24–25 Zoran Milic/iStockphoto; p.25 (top) Library of Congress; p.25 (bottom) Patrick Hard/Shutterstock; p.26 (top) Margaret Stephenson/Shutterstock; p.26 (bottom) Norman Chan/Shutterstock; p.26–27 Cathleen Clapper/Shutterstock; p.27 Pritmova Svetlana/Shutterstock; p.28 (top) Mike Mosall II/Shuterstock; p.28–29 Nicoll Rager Fuller